KEY TO LIFE

AN INTRODUCTORY SKETCH TO RUDOLF STEINER'S

PHILOSOPHY OF FREEDOM

by

Iddo Oberski

Eloquent Books

Eloquent Books
An imprint of Strategic Book Group
P.O. Box 333
Durham CT 06422
www.StrategicBookGroup.com

ISBN: 978-1-60911-865-5

Printed in the United States of America

Book Design: SP

This book is dedicated to all who work for peace by developing their own spiritual freedom. Know yourself!

With thanks to
Karla Kiniger and the members of her
reading group for the many hours of discussion.

TABLE OF CONTENTS

PREFACE

It is a rare experience to come across a book that claims to solve the riddle of life and succeeds in doing so. Rudolf Steiner's Philosophy of Freedom (abbreviated PoF, translation Michael Wilson, Rudolf Steiner Press, London 1999), first written in German in 1898, provides a key to the understanding of life and the world. It opens doors to a kind of knowledge that can form a firm foundation upon which to build all further knowledge. While I cannot (yet) claim to understand every single one of Steiner's ideas, I now have sufficient grasp of it to lead me to the firm conviction that this is the book of the new millennium. It just happens to have been written about one hundred years before its time!

I have come across many people who know about this book, who have even tried to read it, but who have pulled away because of the effort involved in breaking through the philosophical approach and somewhat formal language Steiner uses. Yet, those who do persevere invariably find that there comes a point when confusion begins to dissolve, clarity emerges and real treasures are revealed. Once this point is reached, it seems to become progressively easier to assimilate Steiner's meaning with subsequent readings, each of which is likely to lay bare further layers of understanding.

However, the fact remains that though written for the general public, PoF is not an easy read. This is partly for the reasons outlined above, and partly because Steiner explores his two main questions from a fairly exhaustive range of different perspectives, causing us often to lose sight of the key ideas he develops.

Yet, in the opening chapter he himself also proclaims, in relation to overly complex philosophical treatises on the question of freedom of the will, that all that really matters is "the straightforward train of thought" (p. 4). But PoF is no ordinary philosophical treatise. It is a living, breathing, journey through the landscape of human potential. As such it evokes and necessitates the reader's total engagement, to ensure not merely an understanding of the logical argument, but a first hand experience of the reality of the idea of freedom. So Steiner did not intend this to be an easy read, but carefully crafted his book to draw his readers into the experiences required to understand his argument. Nevertheless, however much I love the PoF itself, I do believe there is a need for a more gentle introduction to it, written in simple, contemporary language.

So the purpose of my short book is twofold: (1) to provide a condensed outline of the main train of thought that runs through the PoF and (2) thereby to inspire readers to take up the study of Steiner's book itself. I am not at all under the illusion that in the following pages I could provide a complete picture of PoF. My book should not be thought of as being a substitute to studying the original; there simply is no substitute for that and my attempt at easing the way in is far from perfect.

8

But if by reading this much shorter sketch you are encouraged to then forge ahead with the study of Philosophy of Freedom itself, the effort of writing this has paid off. For there is much more of value in Steiner's book than the simple train of thought presented here. Steiner's book opens many doors to experiences and insights that are full of life and gives many glimpses of a most fundamental understanding of life.

So here's what to do. Read this introductory book so you get the essence (or bare bones) of the line of thought. Then read and reread the PoF itself, from beginning to end, from the end to the beginning, or pick out specific chapters or passages. Reading and understanding that book is an experience of thinking and through that also a living encounter with the foothills of the spiritual world. However, it is not easy, and Steiner knew this. He remarks more than once that insight into what he is teaching us comes through internal struggle and perseverance, just like insight into any branch of human knowledge comes only after sacrificing time and effort.

To come to understand PoF is indeed a struggle. But it is well worth it. This struggle involves in-depth reading and reflection and if possible, discussion with others. And even though progress may be small, the fruits of every small step towards understanding are sweet indeed! That is not just my own experience, but also of many others I have met over the years and with whom I have shared many hours discussing the content of PoF. They all agree that studying the Philosophy is a real experience. And my book about PoF can never do what a persistent study of the actual book itself can do, but hopefully it helps you make a start.

Over the next decades and centuries, PoF will gain in importance, as the 'New Age' takes root and more and more people refuse to take on a creed handed down to them by their parents. But while rejecting, or simply being ignorant of, one's spiritual heritage is one thing, finding an authentic nourishment for the desire to know the spiritual, rather than to merely believe, is quite something else. The Aquarian Age is supposed to be about thinking for yourself, being independent, being free. The Philosophy of Freedom, though written in the 19th Century, is a guide to the development of an independent thinking that goes beyond most current modes of thinking. It is a guide to a living, feeling, loving thinking that can form the very foundations of human life in the 21st Century and beyond.

In what follows, I have closely followed the chapter structure of the Michael Wilson translation and have focused on the key argument in Part One and the first few chapters in Part Two. Please remember that I have attempted to give a condensed version of Steiner's argument, not my own, but the way I have represented his views is completely my own responsibility. I have tried wherever possible to paraphrase rather than quote Steiner, but often I remain very close to Steiner's own words. This will help you identify our place in the original argument. You may also find it helpful to familiarize yourself with Steiner's earlier book, A Theory of Knowledge Implicit in Goethe's World Conception.

The rest of Part Two of PoF is concerned with a range of far-reaching philosophical questions treated from the perspective of the view developed in part one. However, once the key ideas are clear, these further chapters are relatively easy to come to grips with, despite their somewhat technical nature. Therefore I felt justified in omitting them in this brief sketch.

If nothing else, this book no doubt illustrates the extent of my own understanding or lack of it. Comments, both positive and constructively critical are therefore more than welcome. My email is ioberski@gmail.com

Iddo Oberski, Edinburgh, Hogmanay 2009

"I give myself to the Spirit's revelation
And gain the light of cosmic Being;
The power of thought grows strong and clear
And gives my own true self to me;
By thinking's power the sense of self
Awakens and is freed."

(From Rudolf Steiner's Calendar of the Soul, Translation ©
John B. Thomson 2004)

INTRODUCTION

If you are already perplexed by life and full of questions that you are just craving to answer, then you could skip to the next chapter. Otherwise, let me try and whet your appetite.

What is life?

Is it:

- **?** An accumulation of chemical and physical processes.
- **?** A coincidental non-purposeful self-replicating organic machinery.
- **?** Created by an all-powerful God.

Who am I?

Am I:

- **?** A specimen of a human species, which evolved over millions of years in response to the environment.

? A physically and chemically determined entity driven solely by the need to eat, sleep and reproduce.

? An animal like all other animals.

How can I find out what the world, life and myself are all about?

? We can find the explanation for everything in the world through science.

? Cause and effect only operate within the narrow bounds of the physical.

I have put question marks before these statements to allow some room for openness when it comes to understanding the world. Try to let go of these ideas for a minute and see if you can regain some of the wonder about life and the universe that pre-scientific generations may have had and that is simply based on your experience before learning about science.

Look at a stone. It is hard, solid material. It does not move by itself, nor grow (although some crystals of course do 'grow'). Where do its colors come from? What about its shape? Where did you find it and how did it get there? With a stone we can possibly trace its whole journey as a chain of causal events acting on it. Or can we? There is no drive or movement or change coming from within the stone itself.

Look at a rose, or any other plant, growing in the earth. Look at the colors. The earth is black and brown, an indeterminate mass of decomposed organic matter with only darkness holding it together. Then look at the plant and its flower. A well-organized and growing, living thing, with different shades of green, well defined forms (leaves, thorns, stems etc.) and brightly red or yellow or orange flowers. How is it possible for all this order, colour and growth to emerge out of a dark, undefined, moist mass of earth? It is incredible. Is it simply the sun and rain acting on the earth, producing the plant? No, of course there was a seed first. But the seed produces the plant out of itself, given the right environment for it to do so. Very unlike the stone. The seed is alive.

Look at an animal, your dog, the neighbor's cat, a fox, a blackbird. It is no longer rooted in the earth, but seemingly self-sufficient. Where did it come from? How is it possible for an animal to survive by eating plants or other animals and drinking water? The blackbird eats berries, the fox eats rabbits, the cat eats mice, the squirrel eats nuts, yet they do not take on the form of what they eat. Instead they somehow manage to convert whatever they eat into their own form, like the plant. But the things they eat are themselves alive. They cannot survive by eating earth. But unlike most plants, animals can move and make sounds and feel things, they can form relationships and recognize where they are. How does a mass of chemical and physical processes (there is my scientific thinking again) set a pair of wings in motion? What is it in the fox that makes it capable of looking after its cubs? Plants don't look after their seedlings.

Now look at yourself, a human being. You also need to eat and drink like the animal and you do not take on the form of the things you eat and drink, but keep your own, human form. You also can move and make sounds and feel things. You sleep and wake up being the same person.

But now look at all the things you can ask and wonder about. You can wonder about stones and plants and animals and yourself as a human being. Where does this wondering come from? Do animals wonder about things? Do they think?

15

What is thinking? How do you know if your thinking actually helps you find the truth? Who thinks in you? Is your thinking simply a chemical process in your brain? How is it possible for logic to exist, for one thought to follow from another by necessity? Could you live without thinking? Could you understand anything without thinking?

When it comes to religion, I struggle with the idea that you simply have to believe in God. This is something most religions have in common. You have to take the holy books and the priests at their word that God exists, even if you have no direct experience of God yourself. You have to BELIEVE. And though I can try to see and feel God in everything around me, really if I am honest, I don't see God, or certainly not in the way that I see other things around me. Now of course there are lots of other things I believe without having had first hand experience of it. For example, I believe the newsreader on TV when she says that eight soldiers were killed in Afghanistan. (But I take the weather forecast with a pinch of salt!). And I believe my daughter when she says she had pasta for dinner on her sleepover. But these things are all possible within my personal experience. I know people get killed in wars, in fact my own grandparents were. Also, we regularly eat pasta at home so I know it is possible. It is rather more difficult though to believe that Moses parted the sea, or that Jesus walked on water.

Would it be possible to know the spiritual world in a similar way, with the same certainty that we have in our knowledge of the material world? So that I do not have to believe, but can come to know out of my own experience? I want to be able to relate the mysteries of the world to my own experience, I want to know them and not merely believe in what others tell me. Rudolf Steiner helps us to do exactly this, sketching out the first steps we need to take towards knowledge of the spiritual world, based entirely on our own experience, without needing to believe anything other people tell us. Maybe I am only halfway there, but if nothing else, I now know with certainty that it is possible to achieve this. This is why I love Steiner's Philosophy of Freedom.

HOW TO READ
PHILOSOPHY OF FREEDOM

The Philosophy of Freedom is divided into two parts. Steiner sets out his main ideas in answer to the two fundamental questions he poses, namely "Are we free in our actions?" and "Is there a self-sustaining view of the world that can form the foundation of all our knowledge?" In Part One he essentially develops an argument that leads to a self-sustaining view of the world and provides thereby the foundation for answering the first question, which he then does in Part Two.

My own understanding of the book is continually developing and over time I have become more relaxed about how to read it. Initially, I tried to read it from cover to cover, failing at least three times, though getting slightly further each time. The key I think is not to try and understand every single idea or argument at first, but to read loosely. When you get all confused, just accept it but keep reading. It won't be long before you reach a point where Steiner summarizes, or rephrases the essence of what has gone before, allowing you then to pick up the thread and read on.

Start by reading the prefaces and the additions at the end of some chapters. I find that these often provide just those ideas that somehow remained implicit in the main text or perhaps were developed so deeply that I lose the thread. It is also helpful to just pick out a particular chapter, or section, or even just a paragraph or sentence for in-depth contemplation. Read it, go over the main ideas in your own mind and see if you can really sense the connections being made. Can you experience for yourself the path of thinking that Steiner has laid out for us?

Try not to get bogged down too much in single words or sentences, as often the meaning is more diffusely distributed across larger sections. Sometimes you may find you get really fed up with the book, become irritated by your own lack of understanding or you begin to find Steiner's approach really tedious. It feels like a kind of mental indigestion. Just stop, put the book aside and forget about it. Then a few days, weeks or sometimes even months or years later you find yourself coming back to it after recovering your sense of wonder about life! I always know where my copy is, have often had to lay it aside, give it a rest and digest. Then over time again and again I am drawn back to it, as my soul grows hungry again.

Over time you will find that each reading builds up a new layer of understanding. Then suddenly something will click and give you a sense that this really does provide answers to the riddles of the world. This will then motivate you to keep reading and rereading until the seed of understanding grows roots, a stem, leaves and eventually a flower!

It can also be tremendously helpful to have a small group of people to discuss the book with, as speaking about it and listening to others can progress your own and others' understanding considerably, as well as clarify any misunderstandings. If you live somewhere where there is an Anthroposophical Society, there will very likely be a reading group discussing PoF. But you may wish to set up your own one, because the discussions within the society groups often get drawn towards Steiner's later works. And although his later books are all built on the theory of knowledge he develops in the Philosophy of Freedom, ideas about Karma, Angels, Temperaments and soul anatomy, to name but a few, often creep into the discussion and give the impression of belief, rather than knowledge. You will not find any reference to such entities in the Philosophy of Freedom.

Basic Question

Are we free in our actions or are they all lawfully determined just like the movements of the planets around the sun? The fact is that there are some actions for which we know why we do them and others we just do, without necessarily knowing why. Obviously, if we do not know why we're doing something, it is hard to maintain we are free. And if we briefly look at freedom as in 'freedom of choice', surely any so-called 'free' choice we make can be explained again by some unknown causes, which have determined our choice without us being conscious of them, so then we're not free either.

A deed done in the full knowledge of why we carry it out, of our motivation, is different from one where we do not know why. So freedom has to do not so much with the deed itself. It is about what we know about ourselves in relation to the deed. It is about what we think prior to acting and about how we are consciously motivated to act in a specific way. In other words, freedom is only ever meaningful in the context of beings who think and the question of freedom is therefore intimately tied up with the nature of thinking. We simply cannot understand freedom if we do not first understand thinking. So what is thinking exactly?

DESIRE FOR KNOWLEDGE

As adults we are full of questions and much of our lives hinge upon these questions and their answers. At the same time of course we are beings of nature. Like the animals and plants, we are part of this universe and cannot remember ourselves coming into being. Our bodies carry us through life but nature has given us certain needs that we ourselves need to fulfil, such as the need for food and water, warmth and air. But instead of going through life being satisfied with this, living out our lives with what mother nature provides, we constantly want more. Not only do we want more food and water than we need, we also want things that seemingly we do not really need at all, at least not for our day to day survival. For example we want things that merely give us pleasure. And perhaps most of all we want to understand our world, we want to know why the bus is late, how the tree produces apples, how the sun shines and why plants are green. These are all examples of us wanting explanations for the things and events around us. We could simply not bother with such questions, but we do.

Young children take life as it comes. Only when consciousness dawns in them do they begin to ask questions. But even then they can be satisfied with very different kinds of answers, until they wake up to our way of thinking, our scientific logical perspective which demands explanations that only draw on entities we can perceive with our senses. As soon though as we become conscious in this way, we also become aware of ourselves as entities separate from the rest of the world. Our bodies are made up of matter and thereby belong to nature as all the other things around us.

Yet our thoughts and feelings seem of a different quality, they seem non-material and yet they seem dependent on this material body and its brain. Thoughts and feelings I experience in my self. Amongst the things that confront me is this very sense of self, which seems a constant entity. For when I go to sleep I lose consciousness, but on waking up I am still myself, am still the same person, the same I, and can remember my experiences from yesterday. So there is a clear dichotomy here between me, as spiritual, non-material entity and the material world out there. Yet I know that I myself must be a creature of nature like all other creatures, so that somehow there must be a connection between my non-material self and the material world around me. But how do my thoughts get my body to move, how does matter (my brain) think, how does my self get information about that tree 50 meters away? So although we know we are part of nature, yet in our experience it seems we stand opposite her, for in our mental or spiritual experiences we detect nothing material, while everything else in the world does seem to be made up of matter. How do spirit and matter interact?

This quest has in the past been answered in two different ways, both unsatisfactorily. But it is important to briefly outline these two attempts at explanation here. In one approach we try and find a connection, or bridge, between these two different

26

experiences. How does matter relate to spirit, how does object relate to subject, I to the world? Another approach is to try and show that while we experience self and world in such different ways, really they are somehow manifestations of the same fundamental principle, they are both part of nature, and I have to look for ways in which I can understand the world and myself as material and non-material at the same time.

The first approach is dualism, from the Latin word 'duo', two, as it is a two-world view, one spiritual, one material, and tries to find the bridge between them. The other is called monism, from 'mono', one, and tries to find out how spiritual and material can be co-existent. Each of these has different approaches within themselves, depending on how far certain ideas are followed through.

There are three forms of monism: (1) all is matter and what seems to me to be non-material is an illusion, caused simply by the movements of subatomic particles in my brain. This is pure materialism, that recognizes nothing except physical matter. (2) The opposite is where all is said to be spirit and the matter I perceive is really just spiritual and what we perceive as matter is due to an illusion, everything is just my own mental picture. (3) Finally, there is the view that indeed we have both matter and spirit, but really these two are indivisibly connected everywhere I look. The tree consists of both matter and spirit and so does every other thing, so that when I perceive it I see both at once. Both are present in the one.

These monistic explanations of the world can be discarded fairly simply as follows. If we take the view that all is matter, then all we have to do is to ask how we came to that view in the first place? The answer surely must be that we did this through thinking. So the materialist employs thinking to come to his materialistic views. But thinking is clearly experienced as non-material, which contradicts this form of monism. Of course the materialists would argue, yes, but that thinking is itself a purely materialistic process taking place at the level of electro-chemistry in my brain. Very well, so then it is matter that thinks, for we cannot deny that there is thinking involved in some way or another. So then how does this matter think, and even manages to think about itself? In effect, the materialist just shifts the problem away from the dichotomy between self and world, to the dichotomy between matter and spirit. It is not his own thinking, but the thinking of matter itself that now needs to be connected up to the world, but how this is done is not clear at all. And if my experience of thinking is just an illusion, than I am not at all justified in using this very phenomenon (thinking) to explain anything at all. One cannot come to truth on the basis of an illusory process.

It is somewhat more tricky, surprisingly, to discard the spiritualistic monism. For this view, all is spirit. However, the question is, if all is spirit, how come that I seem to have little part in the creation of the (material) world around me? If the world is of the same nature as my thoughts, then how come it meets me in such a different way? I did not just think up the house across the road, or the cloud in the sky. Neither can I make myself a cup of tea by just thinking it. There is a clear difference between me just thinking something and it actually happening, so the material world does seem to present itself as necessary, as I have little control over it through my thinking alone. I could imagine hearing a sound in the distance and do this so well that it is as if a real sound was indeed present (for me at least). Nevertheless I experience a real sound quite differently from an imagined one. I cannot overcome this difference between real and imagined, I have to acknowledge that there is something outside of me that is of a fundamentally different nature than my thought, so that I am right back to the initial dichotomy of spirit and matter. Thus the world of the senses forces itself upon me in quite a different way than the world of thought, making it difficult to maintain that all is spirit.

Finally, the third form of monism, which combines matter and spirit in one can be discarded simply by the realization that it does not really provide an answer to the dilemma of the two opposing qualities of my experience. Why, if all is a blend of matter and spirit, do I yet experience my thoughts as spirit and the tree as matter? If matter and spirit were blended, why do I not perceive just one quality, how is it that I can distinguish at all between material and spiritual processes?

To come back to the fundamental problem that lies in the experience we have of two opposing worlds, one of matter and one of spirit, the key to its solution is to remember that this whole problem is itself a product of our thinking. Through thinking, we have divided the world into two and then ask ourselves how these two worlds can co-exist, how they can be linked. So right at the location (as it were) where matter and spirit might meet, we stand ourselves. Or rather, right at the moment where spirit and matter become visible as separate worlds, our thinking is active. Yet in this very process of separation also lies the answer to our initial question, as we shall see.

While we perceive ourselves to be separate from the world, not in body, but in spirit, surely even this spirit must somehow be part of nature or must retain something of its source, given that in the end we are, as human beings, creatures of nature, top to toe. Once we have identified what this part of nature is that lies within us, we have the key to understanding better our relationship to the world at large.

Unlike other approaches to the question of matter and spirit, the approach offered by Steiner derives from an investigation into the depth of our own nature. It is for this reason that it may seem to you that this approach is nonscientific and subjective. But this is a preconception, as will become clear. However, if you enter into the line of thought set out by him, you will be able to conclude for yourself that such an inner journey is actually fully justified and objective. And that it provides a viable foundation for understanding our human lives and the world.

The importance of this line of investigation lies not least in the fact that it provides a guide into a world that can only be known through first-hand experience, rather than through external knowledge with ready-made answers. It has to become experiential certainty, without any received wisdom. Steiner takes us by the hand and provides us with opportunities to experience what he means. And if we carefully work with his text, taking firmly hold of those opportunities, the experience will eventually emerge quite naturally. The key focus of this inner journey is an in-depth examination of thinking.

THINKING IN THE SERVICE OF KNOWLEDGE

When we observe events in the world, without employing our thinking, we only perceive them as they occur, as they happen in front of our eyes as it were and as long as we are mere observers, they occur quite without our involvement. Every new occurrence in the world around us is then an event unrelated to everything that happened before it or will happen afterwards. In fact, mere observation would barely even distinguish between different events or things as such.

I can watch how a moving billiard ball bounces onto another and sets it in motion. Without thinking, I can know nothing of the motion of the second ball, until I actually observe it. The whole thing simply happens without my involvement. I just happen to observe it. Once it has happened, I can describe how the second ball moved. If, however, I apply my thinking to these observations, I can then say something about the movements of the second ball before the first one hits it, because I know from experience and from the laws of physics that billiard balls bounce off each other and that the direction and velocity of the first ball can be used to predict those of the second ball when it is hit. In other words, without thinking I observe merely a sequence of unrelated events. But with thinking active I am able to relate different events to each other, in this case the movement of the two balls.

It is important to understand that in this case there are two processes taking place simultaneously: observation of the events and thinking about those events. And while I may have absolutely no control over the observed events, I do have control over the thinking. In fact, I am myself absolutely necessary for thinking to occur. The balls may bounce all they will in my absence, but without me, no thinking will take place. At least it seems to me that my thinking is something I do, rather than something that happens to me, although it is possible that this is just an illusion. But for now we will assume that it is indeed I who does the thinking, so that I actively add something to my observation. This is how I experience it.

Certainly it seems to me that the concepts that I use in my thinking are not given to me in the same way that the events and objects in the world are given to me. It seems to me that the events can come and go without any active engagement on my part, whereas the concepts are added by my thinking, my active engagement. I add concepts and ideas that allow me to make connections between my observations and even to predict the nature of events that have not yet happened, provided I understand the laws governing them.

Without thinking I cannot know anything about the connection between things in the world. It is through my thinking alone that events and things in the world become related or connected to each other. Observation does not give this to me, it requires my thinking. The things in the world look

32

very different to me through observation alone, as opposed to observation in combination with thinking.

Through this insight we may come to realize that observation and thinking must be the starting points for any attempt to understand the world and ourselves in it. Observation alone can never give us the connections between objects and events. Anything that anyone asserts about the world must be either based on observation and thinking or on thinking alone, so that other people can understand it by observing and thinking about the same phenomena, or by thinking through the same thoughts respectively. There can be no doubt that thinking plays an absolutely crucial role in understanding the world.

Surprisingly then, it seems that it is due to the way we, as human beings, are constituted, and not to the world, that for us knowledge of the world comes from two quite separate channels: observation and thinking. I cannot gain the concept 'horse' just by observing a horse, nor can I actually create my observation of a real horse merely by thinking of the concept 'horse'. In our day to day experience observation comes before thinking, but with experience they may become so closely linked that they seem to happen simultaneously. This becomes clear when we realize that I only know that I think by first observing thinking within myself. Similarly, all other processes that I experience in relation to my own body or inner world (as distinguished from the world around me) I first observe before I can think about them. Interestingly, viewed in this way, my inner observations are really no different from my observations of the world around me: for example, I observe and identify my feelings within and the sea out there in a similar way. Both seem given to me. Both require thinking to be added in order to establish any relationships or explanations.

However, when I observe specifically my own thinking

something extraordinary happens. Normally, when I observe the world and myself from day to day, I am not aware of my own thinking. My thinking absorbs me totally and focuses entirely on whatever I observe. When on the other hand, I want to observe my own thinking, I have to somehow step back from my ordinary experience and keep in memory what I thought a moment ago, when I observed that tree outside my window. It is impossible for me to observe and think about the tree, while also observing my own thinking about the tree. I can only do this after I have already done the thinking, because I am totally active in thinking.

So one characteristic of thinking is that it is transparent, unobserved, in our normal everyday life. I have to make a special effort to observe my own thinking, just because it needs my full engagement to come about. And because thinking results from my own activity it is also the only thing in life that I can know inside out. After all, I am doing the thinking and by observing my own thinking I can know exactly how my thinking works, how I relate one concept to other concepts. The way two concepts are related depends entirely on the content of those concepts and on nothing else, irrespective of whether the way I connect them is correct or not. Two concepts are brought in relation to each other purely through their own content, their meaning. This cannot be said for my actions, which, while willed by me, only become known to me first through observation and thinking. I may very well do things without full consciousness, but I can never actively think without full consciousness.

I would like to explain something here that I have struggled with for some time. In our daily lives, we connect concepts with each other often according to our own individual experiences. For example, the concept 'boat' calls up a picture in me of a small vessel, which I used to sail in. For you, the same concept will call up a totally different picture. This is because, as we

34

shall see later on, we have individualized the concept through our experience and in this sense added subjective content to it. Nevertheless, the original concept 'boat' in my mind is identical with the concept 'boat' in your mind and is lawfully connected to other concepts, such as 'hull', 'sea', 'dock' and so on. So I need to learn to distinguish which associations in my mind belong lawfully to the concept, and which belong to my subjective experience. I can subjectively relate any concept to any other concept, for example "bowler hat" and "Winston Churchill" can be associated in my mind. But this is merely a subjective association that has nothing to do with the intrinsic meaning of either concept. On the other hand, "head covering" and "spherical" are two concepts which can be objectively related to "bowler hat", as they are intrinsically connected, albeit in one direction only ("bowler hat" implies "spherical" but not the other way around). This does not matter. What is crucial here is that I can survey the relationships amongst concepts purely on the basis of their content. This brings me to another key aspect of thinking.

This second important characteristic of thinking is that when I reflect on my own thinking I am once again using thinking to do so and thus add nothing new to the observation of my thinking, just more thinking, more of the same. I can examine my own thinking with my own thinking. In fact this is the only way to examine my own thinking, which is what we are after. This contrasts with my experience of everything else in the world, where I have to add something of one particular quality, namely thinking, to something of a totally different quality, namely observations that come to me through my senses. When I observe thinking I can completely see the connections between concepts through their very content, whereas when I observe anything else I first have to add the concepts.

So it seems that in thinking we have found a phenomenon

in the world of which I can state that it is truly self-supportive. I do not need anything besides thinking to investigate my own thinking. Whether this thinking is really my own activity and whether it is a valid way of gaining knowledge about the world remains to be seen. But what is absolutely certain is that to my experience, thinking, as my own activity, is the only thing in this world that I can know fully, without needing to add anything to it that is different from thinking.

It is immaterial at this point whether my thinking is correct, the point is that it exists, that it is. An understanding of thinking then must form the foundation of any further exploration of the world. We must fully understand what it is and where it comes from, before we can decide if it gets us to knowledge. So the next chapters will explore what pure thinking is and what its relationship is to observation and to the being that thinks.

THE WORLD AS PERCEPT

When I, as a fully grown human being, observe the world around me, my thinking immediately becomes active. The concepts that thinking adds to my observations cannot be said to derive from those observations. If the concepts came to me through observing the world, were given to me together with my observations, then I would know the world around me immediately on observing it. That this is not so is borne out by my day to day experience and by the fact that children need to learn the concepts belonging to their observations. For example, a baby may grasp at the moon, not yet aware of the distance to it, or may at first be unable to distinguish between dogs and cats.

What then is a concept? When we observe the world, our thinking adds concepts to these observations. Thus, an ideal element is added to the object we observe. When the object is no longer in our field of observation, the ideal element remains. This is the concept. But concepts never stand in isolation, but are in every direction connected with other concepts. For example, the concept 'horse' may be connected with 'quadruped', 'mammal', 'herbivore', 'hooves', 'species', 'animal' etc. I fit each new concept into the network of concepts I already have. And concepts form a closed system, they are all mutually dependent on each other for their meaning. I cannot get outside this system of concepts at all. I cannot define any concept without using other concepts.

When I hear a sudden noise without my thinking becoming active, I just let the noise pass by, I may not even notice it. When my thinking however does become activated, it first identifies the observation as a noise. It may also see the noise as an effect. Then, the concept 'effect' invariably calls up the concept 'cause' and thus I go on to wonder about and look for the cause of the noise, which may subsequently be found, for example by the observation of a little bird fluttering away, or a dog splashing about in the water.

But we must become aware that the thinking that lights up in me when I observe the world cannot be said to be subjective. It is true that I experience thinking as something going on inside me and therefore not accessible directly to anyone but myself. This may cause me to say that it is subjective. However, this conclusion I can only draw by using my thinking in the first place, which if subjective, may not provide me with the truth of the matter at all. In fact thinking precedes the very distinction between subjective and objective, between subject and object. If I call my thinking subjective, I have already gone through a thought process and thereby used the very process (thinking) that I am wanting to characterize. Instead, thinking lies beyond subject and object and precedes it in time. It can only be truly understood by making it the subject of my inner observation.

After all, it is also through thinking that I set myself as I , as the being who thinks, against the rest of the world. My thinking divides the world into world and I. From this perspective it would therefore also be misleading to say 'It is I who thinks'. Rather, it is my subjectivity, my self, which becomes distinguished through thinking. Did Descartes have this in mind when he proclaimed his famous words "I think, therefore I am"?Thinking comes first, then I and world, or subject and object. In myself as subject, I do experience an entity that continues as such, as myself, from day to day, a constant being that confronts the world, but remains the same being despite changing. My experiences may be broad and varied, but my I remains the same I throughout my life. Thus through thinking, I on the one hand set myself apart from the world, but at the same time it is only through thinking that I can then join all observations in the world together into a unity again.

But how do objects of observation reach me at all and what are they? The only way to get an inkling of this is by imagining the world without thinking. If you were a being with the full ability of your senses but without the ability to think, then what would the world look like to you? It would be a mass of unrelated events and phenomena, objects of observation, forms, sounds and colors (but you would not identify them even as such) and you would have no intrinsic interest in their relationships, their meaning or their substance. It is only through thinking that such objects become identified as entities in themselves and that their relationships light up. And since thinking itself cannot be said to be subjective, these relationships it establishes can also not be said to be subjective.

Yet, on second thought, where can I really identify a sharp division between myself and the world? When I observe a tree out there, the concept 'tree' lights up through my thinking. When the tree is no longer in my visual field, there is nevertheless still something of the tree left within me. I can form a mental picture, however inaccurate or vague, of that particular tree, which has become associated with the concept 'tree' and my self has undergone a change by having this mental picture added to it, in response to the observation of the actual tree. I am changed by retaining a mental memory picture. But in a similar way do my feelings, emotions and acts of will come to me through observation and thinking. When I feel hunger, I only know this by observing the feeling and by the concept 'hunger' lighting up through my thinking. Thus, all these observations, of the outer world as well as of the inner world, come to me through observation and thinking. Steiner uses the term 'percept' to refer to the content of observation before it becomes connected to a concept.

But what is the relationship between the percept and the actual object? If all I have of an object is my mental picture, how do I know that the object really exists? How do I know if the whole world is not merely my own mental picture? And what is the relationship between my mental pictures and the real objects, if they do exist? In answer to this, why would the world be puzzling to me if I were its creator through my mental pictures?

In my experience, the mental picture is what remains after an object of observation has been in my perceptual field and then disappeared from it. I also know from experience that the exact observation I make of the world is to a large extent dependent on my position in time and space and on my bodily organization. If I look at a house from a helicopter, I get a very different picture of it than from inside it or in front of it. If I have limited sense organs, for example I lack the ability to smell, certain observations are not possible for me.

Now again, it is tempting to derive from the notion that our observations are dependent on our sense organs the idea that therefore they must be subjective. It is true that they are determined by our physical organization. But that does not mean that I am their creator. The question really is what role, if any, is played by myself in the bringing forth of percepts. It is simply impossible to answer this by just looking at percepts, because we always are already in the realm of concepts when trying to understand anything, Nevertheless, philosophers have attempted to do exactly this.

For example, from science we know that in my eyes, the image I see gets projected onto the back of the eye and then transformed into a complex of electro-chemical impulses that are sent through the optic nerve to the brain. If I look inside the eye beyond the retina, I will nowhere find anything that resembles the original observation. I can trace the stimuli perhaps to a variety of locations within my brain, but I cannot ever trace how these stimuli then again in the brain become a picture that I actually experience and project onto the object outside me. Yet it might be thought that this proves that our percepts are really only electro-chemical signals in my brain and that these bear no resemblance to the object I seem to observe. Therefore, it seems as if the world dissolves into an illusion, brought forth by my own, unconscious imagination.

But if my observations are merely electro-chemical stimuli, then my observations of this whole process, including the sense organs and what goes on inside them and in the brain, are also just electro-chemical stimuli themselves and can in no way be regarded as giving me an accurate picture of what is really going on. The anatomy of the eye, the electro-chemical signals, the nerve cells and the brain are all objects that I have first perceived and so their existence would have to be questioned as well. And so this whole line of reasoning collapses.

It is simply not possible to understand the world through anything other than thinking and observation. No knowledge whatsoever is possible without thinking and the question of the reality of objects arises only as a result of us artificially

41

dividing what in actuality is one, namely the percept (without the concept) and the so-called 'thing-in-itself'. Therefore to ask what a percept is turns out to be senseless, as a percept is only ever meaningful to us in relation to the concept. We can very well ask what the percept is to thinking, but to ask what it is itself merely suggests that we have not yet fully grasped what it means to stay within actual experience. We have once more based our search on divisions already established by thinking, rather than on our experiential understanding of what thinking really is.

THE ACT OF KNOWING

So we cannot come to a valid understanding of the world by just examining our percepts, the content of our observations. If I think the observed world is just my own mental picture and I cannot know the things in themselves directly, or even if I think that all there is are my mental pictures, and there are not even any things in themselves, I am simply forgetting in all this that I have once more used thinking to reach these conclusions. And the whole question is just if and to what extent my thinking actually gives me valuable knowledge of the world, so I first need to understand thinking, before anything else.

Anything we can say about my observations of the world is first mediated by thinking, it is simply impossible therefore to understand the world by just examining my percepts, I always have to add something to the percepts, namely my thinking! Remember, I have already found out what a world without thinking would be: a meaningless mixture of various forms, colors, movements, without any connections between them. And even this is already a description relying on thinking

43

('form', 'colour' etc. are concepts).

To a so-called 'naïve' consciousness, the observed world is simply real and exists independently of me. Thinking, according to this view, is something unnecessary that we as human beings add quite subjectively to the world, but the world would simply be identical without it. But in fact it is quite arbitrary to make such a distinction between the world out there and the world within me. Given that I can observe my inner world and my thinking in exactly the same way as everything else outside of myself (albeit not through the sense organs), what right do I have to say that only the latter, external, observations really exist? None whatsoever, my inner world is just as much part of the whole world as everything I observe through my sense organs. And this includes thinking itself.

No, the only valid step beyond the idea that the world (now including inner and outer world) has objective existence is to ask how my thinking is related to it. All that I have of the world is percepts, so how is thinking related to percepts? I simply cannot get outside thinking at all if I am trying to understand the world. From a naïve point of view I simply take the world at face value and believe that the objects I perceive are really there and continue to be there just so even in my absence. However, realising that my thinking is as much part of the world as my percepts, I cannot simply close my eyes to it, I must acknowledge that in thinking we have an element of nature as much as in other percepts, although, as said before, usually we do not see the thinking, as it is wholly focused on the percepts. For example, we can say that a seed has the potential to grow into a plant, but only if the right conditions prevail, water, earth, sunlight etc. Similarly, concepts only arise when human consciousness is present. It is as if human consciousness provides the soil in which concepts can emerge, when an observation is sown into it! In other words, without my presence, the ideal (but real), conceptual nature of the world around me simply does not become manifest at all. But since I am of nature, so are the concepts that arise through my thinking.

The tree out there and the concept 'tree' are not separate entities at all, but belong together, even though the percept comes to me separately from the concept. But that in itself is no justification for believing they are separate. When I hear thunder some seconds after I see lightning, I connect the two observations as belonging together as well. Their separation in time does not compel me to think of them as separate phenomena (though their connection has of course been discovered through empirical science and in the past people may well have thought of them as separate events altogether). If no human being would ever observe the tree, then the concept 'tree' would not arise, just like a seed would not sprout if no earth was surrounding it.

Thinking positions itself right in between the world and anything I want to say about the world. And thinking is not merely something subjective, something we human beings add to percepts, but might as well leave out. No, thinking is beyond subject and object and should be considered as much part of nature as the flower growing in the meadow. The concept belonging to the percept comes to me separated from it only as a result of my physical and psychological organization. It does not matter to the flower whether or not a human consciousness confronts it, but when this does happen, the concept 'flower' arises. It does not matter to the seed whether or not it falls into the earth, but when it does, the plant can emerge.

Thus, while the flower still exists when no human consciousness is observing it, it does not exist as 'flower'. Only in connection with human consciousness does the concept 'flower' emerge. So in this sense human consciousness is like another sense organ. It intuits concepts belonging to percepts. When I come across a tree in pitch darkness, I can feel it but not see it. The tree is there, but only part of it is manifest to me. When the sun rises and the light grows, I can see the tree as well as feel it. Similarly, when my thinking weaves into my observation of the tree, I can determine the concept 'tree' to be part of the tree. It is quite immaterial in all this whether or not I have the correct concept belonging to each percept. It is quite possible for my thinking to be erroneous, just like it is possible that my picture of the tree based only on touch is wrong, and different from the visual picture I can add. But it is quite impossible for thinking itself, as a process, to be right or wrong. It simply is, in the same way that other manifestations in nature are.

Furthermore, in my experience concepts have a permanence that percepts do not. I pick a flower and put it in a vase at home. Say it is a daisy. What I see of the daisy changes every day. The petals open and close. After a few days the daisy begins to welt, the petals fall off and so on. My observations change from day to day, the daisy looks different every day and yet it is still a daisy. The concept 'daisy' in other words remains unchanged. Even when the daisy has disintegrated, what remains is the concept of it. So the world out there which I, as naïve realist, think is real, comes and goes and transforms in manifold ways, while that which I, as naïve realist, think to be merely subjective, is actually constant throughout all these changes. It turns out that concepts have a permanence that percepts simply do not have. So in our daily lives, we are actually quite mistaken to see the material world as permanent. It is in fact the ideal world which shows itself to be more solid, as it were, then the material world!

Since we as individuals stand at the periphery of the world in the sense that we did not ourselves create it, but find ourselves within it, we can only grasp it by examining what already is.

46

If we were inseparable from the world, then everything would be known to us in an instant from the moment we came into being. And if we had created each our own world ourselves, we would know it intimately from the start. However, the fact that percepts and concepts come to us more or less one by one is not due to the things themselves, but due to our own organization as human beings. The fact that we experience concept and percept separately is therefore really subjective: it is not due to the things that they reveal themselves to us as a collection of separate characteristics (red, green, tall, prickly) but to our physical and spiritual organization.

So how are we as beings related to all other things in the world? To begin with, I am a percept amongst all other percepts. I observe my inner world and identify this with the I and can enumerate characteristics of myself in the same way that I can describe any other object in the perceived world. But I can also determine myself in relation to the rest of the world by means of thinking. In this case I move from simply identifying aspects of myself that belong to me, to placing my whole self within the world context, through thinking. Remember that thinking is not subjective, but universal, so that through thinking I can lift myself as it were outside myself and begin to understand my place in the world. But I can only do this insofar as I am able to first grasp the essential nature of thinking itself.

So this is another aspect of our two-sided nature: we perceive ourselves as beings amongst all other beings, yet because we think (which is universal) we are the "all-one being that pervades everything" (p.70). Thinking as a force emanating from the centre of the universal world manifests in us, who stand at the periphery. Thinking appears in human consciousness through intuition, just like the percept appears to human consciousness through observation. Knowledge combines percept and concept in human consciousness.

47

Intuition (the gaining of concepts) and observation are the sources of knowledge (p.73). Thus it is senseless to look at percepts only and try to gain a foothold in the world through that. Percepts are only one half of reality, the other half consisting of concepts. All attempts to find relationships in the world are therefore mediated through thinking and as such ideal relationships. Relationships and connections only exist for thinking and it is thinking which provides the ground for finding unity in the world. Similarly, any and all relationships between myself as subject and the world, I can only establish with thinking and are thus ideal relationships.

If it were possible to observe how percepts appear out of nothing, we might then be able to speak of a 'real' link between 'matter' and 'spirit'. However, this will never be possible, as we have seen, as all such relationships would need to be established by thinking and are therefore by necessity ideal relationships. If a table appears in my field of vision, my thinking adds the concept 'table' to the observation. It can also add the concept of 'I' to this observation. I can further retain a picture in my mind of the table and of my 'I' once the table has disappeared from my field of vision. This picture is in fact the only thing I can justifiably call my 'mental picture'. This picture corresponds to the change in my I in response to the actual observation and in this sense it is a subjective percept, that is retained within my perceptible I as a result of observing the objective percept of the actual table. By now looking in more detail at what a mental picture is we'll draw down our whole understanding of our relationship to the world from the domain of thinking into actual life and begin to see how this world view can have profound consequences for our lives.

HUMAN INDIVIDUALITY

So how do I get information about that tree out there? I observe the tree. The tree is a percept. But is the percept representative of the real tree? The sense organs work by ways of electrical stimulation, so is all I can really say about the percept that it is my subjective mental picture? No, once more I am forgetting about thinking. Without thinking, the percept remains simply a percept amongst others and I would simply not be interested in it. Through thinking, I connect the concept 'tree' to this percept. And this thinking in me is not something subjective, but stands beyond subject and object. This thinking is part of the universal cosmic process, as much as the tree is.

The tree and I are both manifestations in the same world, we are of the same kind, we are both of Nature. It is through thinking that I separate myself from the tree, and from the physiological processes that lie between the tree out there and my percept in here. But those processes are themselves percepts and any relationships between them, the tree and myself, all as percepts, have to be established by means of thinking. And thinking is part of the universal world process itself. So it is not at all necessary for something material or physical to move from the tree to me, as in fact tree and me are only separate as long as thinking separates them in a naïve realistic way. As soon as my thinking recognizes what thinking is, tree and I can once more be brought together, be one.

When I see a tree, concept and percept join through thinking. When I then see another tree, the same concept joins this new percept. But when I see exactly the same tree I recognize it as such, because I have formed a mental picture of that particular tree. The mental picture is of course subjective to the extent that it is dependent on my position in time and space. Provided I am able to hold on to such individualized mental pictures, I am able to gain experience of the world. So by relating the concept and percept through my own mental picture I gain an individualized concept of the tree. The mental picture is therefore an individualized concept and all my mental pictures taken together can be called my total experience.

Now besides relating percept to concept through our mental pictures, we also relate concepts to our self, through feeling, and thereby further individualize the mental picture, by associating it with pleasure or displeasure. Thinking and feeling correspond to our two-folded nature in that through feeling we are wholly within ourselves, whereas through thinking we are taking part in something universal, something cosmic. And while immediate experience may suggest that our feelings are much more real and immediate than our thoughts, our own feelings are only real to ourself, whereas concepts have a universal value, beyond the individual. Feelings can of course gain such universal value, if through thinking they are connected to the universal world process.

50

But this is an indirect route, whereas for thinking itself this is a given. Feeling gives to concepts concrete life, through individualized mental pictures. Without feeling, our lives would simply remain within the cognitive realm and while we would be able to link concepts to percepts, they would remain indifferent to us personally. On the other hand, a life of feeling without thinking would contract into itself and become totally isolated from the rest of the world.

ARE THERE LIMITS TO KNOWLEDGE?

We have already seen how we gain knowledge by combining concept with percept. Due to our own constitution or organization the world comes to us through these two different channels of observation and thinking. With the development of observation and thinking, new percepts will emerge and new concepts will be drawn down through thinking. So knowledge will never be complete, or fixed, but will always keep developing and changing. This is the new monistic view developed by Steiner, the view that all is one, that the world only seems to be divided into matter and spirit due to our mental organization and not due to the things themselves.

Dualism closes its eyes to the fact that in thinking we have an element that lies beyond matter and spirit, beyond subject and object. In doing so, it takes the way in which the world comes to us as two completely different worlds, the world of objects and the world of thoughts and then tries to find a way to understand the relationships or links between these two worlds. It then needs to hypothesize for example that what we observe is not what is actually there, but only the subjective result of something our sense organs pick up. This something we can never really know directly, but we can call it the 'thing in itself'.

However, for Steiner's monism, this is not a justifiable view. To it, there are only percepts and concepts. Everything that we try to understand we must first think about, so thinking is primary. There is no need to speculate about the 'thing in itself' because everything there is to know, ever, is given through percept and concept while the 'thing in itself' is by definition unknowable, because it is a product of erroneous thinking. For this monism, all questions pertaining to the world can be answered through observation and thinking and there is no need to hypothesize worlds of which we can have no direct knowledge. Thus while dualism certainly sets barriers to our knowledge, claiming that we can never know the things in themselves directly, Steiner's monism rejects this view.

THE FACTORS OF LIFE

If all we did was observe and think, then we would be able to determine the world and ourselves solely through cognition. However, as said before, we also have feeling and will (the impulse for action). When we form a mental picture of an object that temporarily lies within our field of observation, we have individualized a concept by connecting it to our own unique perspective. This perspective includes feelings. The same is true for the mental pictures we form of ourselves. In these mental pictures we have a relationship, through thinking, of the self to itself, determining our own personality.

However, the feelings that we bring into connection with the concepts are themselves percepts, although they are percepts emerging in our inner world, as opposed to the percepts coming to us from the world around us. A naïve realist would take these feelings as real in the same way that he/she takes the percepts of the outer world as real. Because of this, to a naïve realist feelings seem real, as opposed to thinking, which seems subjective. Mysticism is based on feeling and attempts, instead of understanding the world though thinking, to develop a oneness with the world though feeling. In this sense, the mystic is a naïve realist. But from our monistic point of view, the feelings that arise in us must be seen as percepts and therefore as only one half of reality, to be complemented by concepts through thinking.

So it is only through thinking that my feelings may obtain universal significance, Without thinking, they are a purely individual affair. Thinking, feeling and willing are all spiritual activities, but only in thinking are we ourselves wholly active. Feelings to a large extent seem to come to me without my conscious control. Acts of the will, when fully conscious, are initiated through thinking and when not, they become accessible to consciousness only as percepts, which again need first to be combined with concepts before they become meaningful.

THE IDEA OF FREEDOM

Lets bring together our new understanding of the nature of thinking with human action itself. To begin to understand the idea of freedom, it is absolutely necessary for us to first struggle through to the insight of what thinking really is. And this we can only do by introspection, by carefully observing our own thinking, without adding any extraneous elements to this. We must transform thinking into experience. When we observe the world, concepts are added to the percepts, we can know nothing of the world except indirectly through our thinking. But when we are in the process of observing our own thinking, the concept of our prior thinking becomes itself a percept for our subsequent thinking. And so concept and percept merge and we experience a self-sustaining spiritual activity in which we know our thinking directly, rather than indirectly (as with everything else in the world). This can only be experienced. However, as Steiner indicates, coming to this understanding ourselves may take some time and effort. The process by which my thinking brings concepts into consciousness is intuition.

Once we really understand what thinking is, we can then go back to consider human freedom from this newly gained perspective. When is a human act really free? We act with various degrees of freedom. Steiner does not say that all our actions are free or unfree. In our daily lives, some of our actions are free, while others are not. But we now understand that freedom of action can only really be if there is freedom of thinking, in other words if the action is driven by a thinking that has not been conditioned by my prior experience, my bank of mental pictures or by the immediately given world of percepts. I may of course consciously take all of these into account in any particular situation. But my actions must not be determined by any of these.

We can distinguish between four levels of action, according to the extent to which spiritual freedom lies behind such actions:

The least free are those actions that derive from instinct, where a percept leads directly to an action, without the intermediary of feelings or mental pictures. Such are the actions related to our basic instincts for survival and reproduction. At the next level we act in response to feelings associated with certain percepts, such as pity, pride, shame and so on. I see a beggar in the street and my compassion is evoked, or my sense of guilt or obligation, and I give him money.

The third level of action is where we act according to certain of our mental pictures. For example, I notice that someone is behind me when I leave a shop. The mental picture of holding the door open for the person behind pops into my mind and I act accordingly. The fourth level is where we act purely on the basis of our intuited concepts. We act out of true freedom. In such a case, a situation is evaluated objectively by direct intuition out of the world of concepts, and only our thinking determines what course of action I, as a unique individual at this time and in this place, will take to achieve the best outcome. In this my concepts are not conditioned by any percepts or prior experience (although I may take these into consideration) and derive directly from the world of ideas. I am now no longer acting in a way that is bounded by my own subjectivity, but in harmony with the cosmos.

CONCLUSION

Steiner goes on to explain how it is impossible for two people who act out of true individual freedom, to not agree with one another, or to work against each other. He also explores in some detail the value of life, optimism and pessimism and the notions of moral imagination and moral technique, building on the newly gained understanding of the nature of thinking and freedom explored in the first part of the book and sketched above. Please refer to the original book for these explorations.

All that remains to be said here is that a careful and unbiased inner exploration of thinking can in time reveal to us that we are more than just physical beings, that our thinking rises up above subjectivity and objectivity and that through thinking we can connect all that is in the world around us and can place ourselves solidly within the midst of this world. There can be no externally imposed laws, nor any personal gods or unseen powers to the person who is truly free. Everything needed for an understanding of the world is to be found within the world, but this world includes of course my own inner self and my thinking, which connects me to the cosmos. Grasping the true nature of thinking then leads to the view that through it we are truly engaged in the spiritual world. This spiritual world is now no longer some kind of mystical, vague, never-to-be-known universe, but part of the very world in which we, as human beings, live. It is this world which Steiner explored in great detail in his subsequent works.